Women Who Dared

Illustrations by Jackie Denison

Library of Congress Number: 79-13718

1 2 3 4 5 6 7 8 9 0 83 82 81 80 79

Printed and bound in the United States of America.

Library of Congress Cataloging in Publication Data
McLenighan, Valjean.
    Women who dared.
    Bibliography: p. 48.
    SUMMARY: Presents brief biographies of prominent
women, including Margaret Bourke-White, Diana Nyad,
Janet Guthrie, and Kitty O'Neill.
    1. Women—United States—Biography—Juvenile lit-
erature. [1. United States—Biography] I. Denison,
Jackie. II. Title.
HQ1412.M27   301.41'2'0922 [B] [920]   79-13718
ISBN 0-8172-1375-9 lib. bdg.

WOMEN WHO DARED

Valjean McLenighan

RAINTREE PUBLISHERS
Milwaukee • Toronto • Melbourne • London

CONTENTS

INTRODUCTION

What would it have been like to be the only woman at the front lines during battles in World War II?

Can you imagine disguising yourself as a man, to be able to work and earn enough money to support your children?

What must it be like to drive a race car at speeds above 180 miles per hour?

Do you think you could swim without stopping for six hours a day, and more — swimming distances thirty-two miles and greater?

Can you imagine not being able to hear and yet choosing to fall off of buildings and even set a record for speed on land in a jet car?

And, if you were forty-five and a teacher in the late 1800s, do you think you might have considered changing careers and becoming a mountain climber?

Each of these things has been done by one of the women in this book. They are all women who have wanted a life of adventure. Some of them risked their lives in their line of work, and some of them risked just their reputations.

For their own reasons, these six women have dared to take chances to enable themselves to spend their lives doing the things they chose to do.

MARGARET BOURKE-WHITE

A woman who lives a roving life must be able to stand alone.
You set your own ground rules, and if you follow them, there
are great rewards.

Margaret Bourke-White

The torpedo hit with a dull thud, and the sudden tilting of the troop ship threw Margaret Bourke-White from her bunk. She dressed quickly, grabbed her camera bag, and worked her way through masses of soldiers to the ship's top deck.

The midnight sky was brilliant with a full moon, but there wasn't enough light to take pictures. Margaret heard the order to abandon ship. As she scrambled down the sloping deck toward the lifeboat station, she couldn't help planning the pictures she would have taken if only it had been daylight.

As a war correspondent for *Life* magazine during World War II, Margaret was on her way to cover the Allied invasion of North Africa when her ship was torpedoed. As long as her mind was on her work, she was fine. But as she stood in line to board the lifeboat, she suddenly noticed that her mouth was dry. "Never in my life had I felt such dryness," she wrote later. "This must be fear."

Margaret's photographs and stories in *Life* magazine entertained and informed readers for more than thirty years. Her career took her around the world, recording the rush of modern history. She photographed the famous — including Josef Stalin, Winston Churchill, Franklin Roosevelt, and Mahatma Gandhi. And, her camera probed the faces of the not-so-famous — soldiers, victims of droughts and floods, workers — people whose stories showed the human side of great events.

During World War II, Margaret went into battle and even flew on combat missions in order to cover the stories about the war. She also wrote about India's struggle for independence and about the war in Korea. Then, tragically, Parkinson's disease forced her attention from world conflicts to a life-and-death struggle with her own body.

Margaret was born in New York City in 1906. Her parents, Joseph and Minnie Elizabeth (Bourke) White, thought it was important to teach their children to be fearless. On long nature hikes with her father, an engineer and inventor, Margaret was encouraged to explore and climb up high.

Margaret Bourke-White started her career by taking pictures of buildings and landscapes in Cleveland, Ohio. At a later point in her career, she accepted other assignments, including photographs to be used on magazine covers. But her real love was for the Cleveland Flats. The sprawling industrial area on the Cuyahoga River seemed to her a perfect subject for photography. She saw strength and beauty in industrial forms — bridges, barges, and the huge belching smoke-stacks of the steel mills that ringed the area.

Every night for five months, Margaret and her friend Alfred Bemis prowled the catwalks of the Otis Steel Company, trying everything they could think of to capture on film the dramatic process of making steel. No one had ever taken pictures of the inside of a mill.

While Margaret focused her camera on an object, Bemis held up huge magnesium flares to do the job a flash bulb or strobe light would do today. The heat from the furnaces in front of them was strong enough to blister the varnish on Margaret's camera. She was not shy about placing herself in daring situations to be able to take photographs. Climbing into an overhead crane so she could aim her camera down into a vat of molten steel was just one of many dangerous acts she performed while taking pictures.

Margaret's pictures caused a sensation at the office of *Time* magazine in New York. Publisher Henry Luce was planning a new magazine at that time. For *Fortune* magazine, he wanted the most dramatic photographs of industry that had ever been taken. He wanted to develop a new way of telling stories. His goal was to publish a magazine in which pictures would be as important as words. Henry Luce needed a talented photographer for the magazine. It was the perfect job for Margaret. She joined the staff of *Fortune* in the spring of 1929 and soon was photographing stories on everything from raising orchids to making cars.

In her early years as a photographer, Margaret was more interested in photographing machines than people. But her ideas began to change when she covered the drought of 1934 for *Fortune*. From the Dakotas in the north to Texas in the south, the land was scorched, withered, and dead. Thousands of farmers, defenseless against the forces of nature, were left ruined and bewildered. Margaret felt that she had to tell their story through her photographs. She began to feel a need to use her camera to better understand her fellow Americans. In 1936, she had two wonderful opportunities to do this.

Henry Luce was planning another new magazine. The subject matter of *Life* magazine would be as broad as its title. The success of the magazine would greatly depend on photographs which would show, among other things, how world events and other forces affected the lives of individual people.

While *Life* was still in the planning stages, Margaret worked with writer Erskine Caldwell on a book about the lives of poor farmers and other people living in the South. Margaret and Erskine

Margaret Bourke-White (left) is standing next to her view camera during a visit to Hollywood. Actress Ann Harding is on the right.

Caldwell traveled hundreds of miles through states where cotton and tobacco were grown — from South Carolina to Arkansas and Louisiana.

The combined efforts of writer and photographer resulted in the book *You Have Seen Their Faces*. It showed a side of the South that few Americans were aware of — the grinding poverty of the Southern tenant farmers and the hardships, misery, and despair they experienced. The book was a success. The blending of words and pictures was hailed as a new art form. Most importantly, however, *You Have Seen Their Faces* stirred the

U.S. Congress to pass laws to ease the poverty of Southern farm workers.

From its first issue, Margaret was involved with a magazine which had a lasting effect on American photography. During her long career with *Life*, she photographed just about every imaginable kind of story. She had a journalist's knack for being in the right place at the right time. She exposed the horrors of child labor in Jersey City and traveled to the Arctic for a picture story, where she was marooned for two days on an island 300 miles from civilization.

When America entered World War II, Margaret put on the uniform of a war correspondent. She survived a torpedo hit, flew with airmen on a bombing mission, and experienced all the major campaigns of the war while covering stories at the front lines. She was the only American photographer in Moscow when it was bombed by the Germans. And, when General Patton's Third Army reached Buchenwald, Margaret was there to photograph the horrors of the Nazi death camp.

She was on an assignment in Japan, in 1952, when she became faced with the greatest battle of all. She couldn't ignore the aching in her leg any more, or the loss of balance when she would rise from a sitting position. When she returned to the U.S., the problems continued and she finally went to see a doctor.

When Margaret learned that she had Parkinson's disease, there was no known cure. She just knew that the disease attacked the body's control of its muscles. Although no cure existed, doctors told her that she could, at least, control the progress of the disease by exercising.

Muscle by muscle, Margaret fought her illness. She wadded up countless sheets of newspapers to exercise her hands and fingers. Her arm muscles grew so tight she had to force them to swing. She taught herself to walk again when every step was an effort and then spent long, weary months walking four or more miles every day.

Margaret would not accept the fact that she had an incurable disease. She believed that if she could keep herself in the best possible physical condition, scientists would discover a cure. The lucky timing that had blessed her career as a photographer came through for her again. In the early 1950s Dr. Irving S. Cooper found a new method of treating Parkinson's disease. Two operations within two years resulted in a stunning victory for Margaret after her ten-year battle against the disease.

For the most part, Margaret's life was devoted to her career. She did marry two different times — first, to a fellow college student for two years; and, later, to Erskine Caldwell for five years. "One life isn't better than the other," she wrote. "Just different."

But Margaret Bourke-White, who died in 1971, was glad she chose a life of high adventure. "A woman who lives a roving life must be able to stand alone," she said. "You set your own ground rules, and if you follow them, there are great rewards."

Margaret Bourke-White is shown in 1957 before boarding a plane on the way to an assignment.

MRS. E.J. GUERIN

Whether Mountain Charley was one unique young woman or several interesting young ladies masquerading in men's clothing cannot be determined . . . one or all of the Mountain Charleys were seeking freedom from the repressions of the Victorian Age.

Fred M. Mazzulla and William Kostka

The once-green Missouri field was littered with the bodies of dead and wounded soldiers from both armies of the Civil War.

Dr. Jesse Terry, of the Confederate Shelby's Brigade, looked down at the wounded Union soldier, who was unconscious. Even though the soldier was a "Yankee," the doctor decided he couldn't leave the young man to bleed to death.

The doctor treated the soldier's shoulder and leg wounds. Imagine his surprise when he discovered that the wounded soldier — Private Charles Hatfield, orderly to Union General Curtis — was a woman.

Private Hatfield awoke the next day and knew that the doctor who treated the wounds would have learned her true identity — she was a woman posing as a man in the Union army.

When Dr. Terry approached Private Hatfield that same day, he bent down to confide, " . . . your secret is safe with me until you are able to tell me your story."

And during the long days of her recovery Mrs. E.J. Guerin — known as Mountain Charley, also known as Charles Hatfield — told Dr. Terry her story.

Of all the characters who roamed the country in the mid 1800s, Mountain Charley is one of the most astonishing. She was born in New Orleans; she married when she was thirteen years old; and a few years later her husband was killed. She was left with two babies to care for. Unable to find well-paying work as a woman, she put on men's clothes to earn a living. The young widow also vowed to revenge her husband's murder. A man named Jameison had been tried and convicted of the crime. But he had managed to escape before the hanging.

Charley looked "like an overgrown boy," according to a later newspaper account, and with her husky voice she soon found a job as a cabin boy aboard the *Alexander Scott*. The riverboat sailed the Mississippi between New Orleans and St. Louis.

15

During the next four years Charley worked at many different jobs on the river. But no one ever discovered that she was a woman. Friends of Charley's were taking care of her children. Once a month she put on women's clothes to visit them secretly in St. Louis.

When Charley grew tired of the river, she went to work on the Illinois Central Railroad as a brakeman, a train crew member who inspects the train and helps the conductor. Every so often she took a few weeks off to spend with her son and daughter. On one visit to St. Louis, she spied Jameison, the man who killed her husband, on the street. That night she slipped out, in men's clothes, and found him in a poker game. She waited until the game was over and followed Jameison to a sidestreet. In the shootout that followed, Jameison was wounded in the left arm. Charley was found the next morning with a gunshot wound in her thigh.

By the spring of 1855 she was well enough to set off for California — the Promised Land of Gold. Again she disguised herself as a boy. Charley was the only woman in a wagon train of sixty men, fifty oxen, twenty mules and ten cows, all driven west by gold fever.

The journey took all spring and summer and into the fall. Charley kept a diary along the way. On June 6, 1855, she wrote: "Pass many (wagon) trains today. In the evening a tremendous thunder storm . . . It is my watch and I find it a terrible time." The trail west was littered with abandoned wagons, food, clothes, tools, and wornout horses and mules left to die. On July 5, Charley wrote: "Saw many dead cattle along the road — at least twenty-five per day. Here I shot an antelope — my first . . . The company said I did well for a green boy of eighteen."

In November, 1855, Charley reached Sacramento, California, where she took a job in a saloon. Within six months she owned the place. A year later she sold it for $2,500.

With her profits she returned to St. Louis to spend a few months with her children. Almost two years to the day from her first journey to California, Charley set out again.

Charley's second trip was even rougher than the first. In a fight with the Snake Indians along the Humboldt River, Charley was wounded in the arm. More than a hundred of her cattle died before they reached California.

Still, Charley bought a small ranch in the Shasta Valley and made some other wise investments. Within a few years she returned to St. Louis $30,000 richer. After another long visit with her children, she struck out to trade with the Indians along the Platte River. When gold was discovered in Pike's Peak country, Charley headed for Colorado.

It was there she became known as Mountain Charley. For a while she tried her hand at mining gold. But her real talent was for running a business — this time a "Bakery and Mountain Boys Saloon." For two years Mountain Charley lived and worked in Denver, Colorado, and no one suspected her true sex. But in 1859 a chance meeting with her old enemy Jameison changed all that.

Charley was following a narrow trail in the mountain when Jameison rounded a bend ahead of her. Charley knew him at once and shot him three times before he could gain cover. A couple of nearby hunters heard the shots. Jameison confessed to murdering Charley's husband and told them what he knew of Charley's past.

Charley's story spread all over Colorado. Though people knew her true identity, she continued to dress and do business as a man. But her newly-won fame was not entirely welcome. Leaving her "Bakery and Mountain Boys Saloon" in good hands, she worked her way down to New Mexico as a "mule whacker," where again she could pose as one of the boys. Mountain Charley next led a government wagon train to Kansas and moved from there to Iowa, where, as Charles Hatfield, she joined the Union Army in 1862.

As a clerk at headquarters of the Iowa Cavalry, young Hatfield made herself so useful that she soon became an aide to General Curtis. Dressed as a farm girl selling eggs, private Hatfield made frequent visits to nearby rebel camps to learn what "he" could about enemy plans. No one in the Union army knew "he" was a woman.

General Curtis was well pleased with his aide's success as a spy. "Why, even I would never know you for a lad in that getup," he used to chuckle.

The night before she was wounded, Charley was sent to spy on the famous General Shelby's

Brigade. The rebels were camped on Missouri's Blue River.

Charley was able to learn some important information and returned to the Union lines safely. In the next day's battle the tide turned against the rebels. Charley was wounded in the shoulder and leg.

By the time she got back to her outfit, new orders awaited her. She was promoted to the rank of lieutenant, and General Curtis presented her with an officer's sword and uniform. She served faithfully on his staff until the end of the war.

Perhaps the horrors of war had been too much for her. Perhaps she simply had had enough of a man's life. For reasons known only to her, she settled in Iowa, resumed the clothing and behavior then thought "normal" for a woman, and eventually married and had four more children. She lived quietly for the rest of her life as a farmer's wife.

There are many different accounts of the life of Mountain Charley. Some historians say she was a legend and that it is difficult to separate the facts of her life from the fiction. Many different women claimed to be Mountain Charley and stories of each one's version of the life she led as Mountain Charley were printed in frontier newspapers. The version you have read is based on the autobiography of Mrs. E.J. Guerin, which she titled *Mountain Charley; or the Adventures of Mrs. E.J. Guerin, Who Was Thirteen Years in Male Attire.*

JANET GUTHRIE

A driver is primarily a person, not a man or a woman . . . I am a race car driver who happens to be a woman.

Janet Guthrie

Each year since 1911, the top drivers and cars in America have raced against each other at the Indianapolis 500-mile race. Ray Harroun was the first winner, driving his Marmon *Wasp* at the breakneck speed of 74.59 miles an hour. The list of "Indy" champions grew to include such greats as Gaston Chevrolet, Wilbur Shaw, Bill Vukovich, Parnelli Jones, Mario Andretti, Al Unser, and A.J. Foyt.

By 1976, a driver had to average 180 miles an

hour just to *qualify* for the grueling 500-miler. Almost 2,000 racers had answered the famous Indianapolis starting call: "Gentlemen, start your engines!"

That's right — *gentlemen*. Not one of those 2,000 drivers had been a woman.

But Janet Guthrie changed all that in 1977. On Sunday, May 29, the race began a little bit differently.

"In company with the first lady ever to qualify at Indianapolis — gentlemen start your engines!"

Janet Guthrie was born in Iowa City, Iowa, on March 7, 1938, and grew up in Miami, Florida. Thanks to her father, an airline captain, she learned to fly a Piper Cub airplane at the age of thirteen. Janet earned her pilot's license when she was seventeen. And she later became a flying instructor. By 1960 she had a bachelor's degree in physics from the University of Michigan.

Janet then went to Long Island, New York, to work as an engineer for the Republic Aviation Corporation. In 1965, she heard that the National Aeronautics and Space Administration (NASA) was starting a program to train women astronauts. She thought it would be great to fly spaceships and tried out at once. Janet was among the four women who passed the first group of tests. But then she was cut from the program because she had only four years of college.

Janet had to content herself with racing sports cars. As a teenager, she had promised herself that someday she would own a Jaguar. She wasn't able to make good on it until she had been working for a couple of years. Finally, in 1962, she put down her savings on a nine-year-old Jaguar XK-120.

Janet wanted to drive a car as well as she handled a plane. So she took time off from work to go to a driving school in Lime Rock, Connecticut. One of her teachers was Gordon McKenzie, a former professional driver. He thought she had the timing, the courage, and intelligence to make a fine sports car racer.

McKenzie's encouragement was all Janet needed to trade in her car for a used Jaguar XK-140. Her old car had been built for street driving. But the new car was designed to race.

If racing was going to become a serious commitment for Janet, she knew she would have to learn how to repair her new Jaguar. Such a finely tuned machine can break down after only a few hours at very high speeds, and Janet didn't have the money to hire mechanics.

She decided to take the engine apart and then put it back together. Her only guide was a service manual, which she said looked "like Greek" when she first started working on the engine. For three months in the middle of winter, Janet came home from work every night and went outside to the unheated barn where her car was. She worked by flashlight in the cold. By the time she finished, she knew her engine as well as any experienced mechanic.

Janet joined the Macmillan Ring-Free Motor Maids in 1966. This all-woman sports racing team was sponsored by the Macmillan Ring-Free Oil Company. The team included Rosemary Smith, Europe's leading woman driver, and Liane Engeman from Holland. Among the Americans were Smokey Drolet, Suzy Dietrich, and Donna Mae Mims. Janet raced with the Motor Maids for five years. Much of that time she was team captain.

The Motor Maids were successful from the start. Their first race was the 1966 Daytona Beach endurance contest — a grueling twenty-four hour drive. They entered two cars, Janet, Suzy, and Donna Mae drove one; and Smokey and Rosemary raced the other. Both cars lasted the entire twenty-four hours. Smokey and Rosemary placed eleventh, and Janet and her group followed in twelfth place.

Driving for Macmillan, and later for Goodyear Tire and other sponsors, Janet handled a lot of different cars. The list includes Chevrons, Austin-Healeys, Sunbeams, Mustangs, Camaros, and Toyotas. She raced at Bridgehampton, Daytona, and Sebring — some of the racing sport's greatest tracks. Janet won the North American Road Racing Championship in 1973. Two years later she beat twenty-seven men drivers in a race for the Vander-bilt Cup. She also won the Bridgehampton 400.

Late in 1975, a championship car builder named Rolla Vollstedt put in a call to the SCCA. He planned to enter two cars in the next Indianapolis 500, he said. Veteran Dick Simon would drive one of them. And Vollstedt wanted a woman to drive the other. Without hesitating, club officials recommended their top woman driver — Janet Guthrie.

Janet Guthrie smiles from her racing car just after she qualified for the Indy-500 in 1977. She was the first woman to drive in that race.

Then, suddenly, Vollstedt invited her to drive a championship car — not just in any old race, but in the Indianapolis 500! Janet was thrilled. She said yes right away, before Vollstedt could change his mind.

Vollstedt planned a series of secret speed tests for Janet in February, 1976. His long-time driver, Dick Simon, would watch over the testing. But Dick Simon didn't like his boss's choice of a second driver, and he'd be ready to pounce on any mistakes. If Janet passed the tests, she'd drive one of Vollstedt's cars in the Trenton 200. If she did well at Trenton, USAC would let her try for a spot at Indianapolis.

Ten days before the speed test, Janet broke a bone in her foot while exercising. Just before flying to the Ontario Speedway, near Los Angeles, California, Janet soaked her cast in water to break it off. Then she wrapped her foot in Ace bandages. Dick Simon couldn't argue with such a fierce desire to succeed. And Janet's ability on the track won him over in a few days.

She had passed her first test with flying colors. But when Vollstedt announced his plan to enter Janet in the Trenton 200, a storm of protest broke out among the men who were planning to drive in the Indianapolis 500.

Bobby Unser, a two-time Indianapolis winner, said he had nothing against women drivers. But he and the other men had learned their business on the "Championship Trail" — a tough series of races held each year around the country. Unser said that Janet's entry was just a publicity stunt.

But when the race was over, the men were talking differently. Janet captured fifteenth place — seven slots higher than Bill Vukovich and three places above the famous A.J. Foyt.

Janet did beautifully on her rookie test in Indianapolis. But her car was giving her trouble. Car builder Vollstedt replaced the engine four times, but the *Bryant Special* just wouldn't go faster than 171 miles an hour. A speed of 180 was needed to qualify. Janet and the crew tried everything they could think of. But a week before the big event, they were forced to admit that the *Special* wasn't special enough to race at the Indianapolis.

That night, alone in her motel room, Janet could hardly bear the disappointment. To have come so close to qualifying — it was almost more than she could take.

But then her life took another unexpected turn, as it had when Vollstedt asked her to drive for him. A bank vice-president named Lynda Ferrari flew to Indianapolis with an offer for Janet. Could she sponsor Janet in the World 600 stock car race?

Like the true professional she is, Janet accepted the challenge. She had never driven a stock car, and she faced the same kind of criticism that had flared before she passed the test for the Trenton 200.

With only a week to learn a new track, new car, and new kind of racing, Janet didn't spend much time worrying about her critics. On the day of the race, the track temperature reached 130 degrees.

Janet proved she could take the heat when she finished fifteenth in the race. Twenty-three other cars had dropped out before the race was finished.

By the end of the year, Janet had won more than $8,000 in NASCAR prize money. In 1977, she drove nineteen Grand National stock car races and was named top rookie in both the Daytona 500 and the Richmond 400. She had pioneered NASCAR racing for women. But her heart was still set on Indianapolis.

Janet and Vollstedt started early in 1977 to prepare for Memorial Day — the day of the Indianapolis 500. They had a new, faster car, the *Lindsey Hopkins Lightning*. In it, Janet qualified with a speed of 188.403 miles an hour. On Sunday, May 29, Janet Guthrie made racing history as the first woman to drive in the Indianapolis 500.

Just as on her first try at Indianapolis, Janet's car quit long before she did. Engine trouble forced her out of the race after only twenty-seven laps. Janet finished twenty-ninth out of thirty-three cars.

Janet was back at "Indy" again in 1978. This time she placed ninth, completing 190 laps in her *Wildcat-SGD*. In a year's time, Janet moved up twenty slots closer to the lead. So don't be surprised if the headlines after one Memorial Day read: "GUTHRIE WINS AT INDY!"

DIANA NYAD

What interests me about marathon swimming is that it tests the human spirit. The real issue behind reaching the other shore is . . . the strength of the human will.

Diana Nyad

When she was ten, Diana Nyad wrote an essay called "What I Will Do for the Rest of My Life." She estimated that she had about seventy years to plan for. "I want to see all the countries in the world and learn all the languages," she wrote. "I want to be the best in the world at two things . . . a great athlete and . . . a great surgeon . . . . I need to practice every day. I need to sleep as little as possible. I need to read at least one major book every week. And I need to remember that my seventy years are going to go by too quickly."

In the twenty years since she wrote those words, Diana has already reached several of her goals. She has been around the world six times and has been a world champion long-distance swimmer. She is working for her Ph.D. degree from New York University.

Diana was born in New York City and raised in Fort Lauderdale, Florida. She started to swim when she was six months old. Her natural ability, combined with an iron will, made her a champion swimmer while she was still in junior high school.

Until she was sixteen, Diana was awake every day before dawn for a two-hour workout. Following the morning exercise, she went to school, allowed another hour for sprints at lunchtime, and after school worked out for yet another two hours. Training during the summer was even more concentrated. Often Diana's eyes would swell from spending so many hours in the pool, and her mother would bathe them in ice water.

In the summer after her junior year, 1966, Diana developed a heart ailment. After months of bed rest and staying indoors, she was so weak it took her a full year to recover. Her hopes for the 1968 Olympics were smashed.

Disappointed with her "failure," Diana's first year of college was eventful. At Emory University in Atlanta, Georgia, her energy that had gone into years of strict self-control exploded in a series of college pranks, which included jumping out of a fourth-story window with a parachute. She was expelled from Emory and returned home for a while.

In 1970, Diana enrolled at Lake Forest College near Chicago, Illinois. This time she took her studying more seriously and became an honor student. She also began training to become a marathon (long-distance) swimmer. Diana churned through mile after mile of cool lake water — six hours of swimming a day. In July, 1970, she entered her first professional race — a 10-miler in Lake Ontario.

Diana broke the women's world record for the swim. For the next five years she went to almost every race on the pro tour. The season began in mid-January, with a race in Australia. Then the swimmers went to Argentina, the Caribbean, and Europe. Autumn races were held in Canada, America, Egypt, and Lebanon. Despite this busy racing schedule, Diana managed to graduate with honors from Lake Forest and complete all the courses for her doctoral degree in comparative literature.

Marathon swimming is one of the toughest sports in the world. Tossed by waves for hours on end, the swimmer often endures violent seasickness. The cold temperature of the water can be a problem, too. Once Diana almost drowned when, not knowing the temperature, she forced herself into forty-degree water for a training swim. The marathon swimmer burns up calories at the rate of up to 3,000 an hour. Diana lost twenty-four pounds in one forty-hour swim in the North Sea.

As if the physical strain is not enough, the mind begins to wander after a few hours in the water. On long-distance swims, Diana's goggles fog up, making it difficult to see, and her sense of taste and smell are lost. Her hearing is dulled by several layers of swim caps, and her sense of touch is numbed by the cold. Without information from the senses, a swimmer begins to imagine things.

For example, once Diana thought she was being attacked by sea gulls, and her trainer had to pretend to beat them off with an oar.

Though she was a world champion marathon swimmer and had broken several records in the sport, no one except her fellow swimmers and a few loyal sports writers and fans had ever heard of Diana Nyad. In 1975, she left the pro tour and decided to strike out on her own as a solo swimmer. She was tired of working so hard and being so poor and unknown.

A solo swim around Manhattan Island on October 6, 1975, set a new record of seven hours and fifty-seven minutes and made Diana an instant celebrity. She was front-page news, and the top story on all the local television and radio news reports. She started to write for national magazines and appeared on several television shows. For the first time, she was able to put some money in the bank after paying the rent.

Her next challenge was a double crossing of the English Channel, scheduled for late summer, 1976. No other woman had ever done it. Just for trying the swim, Diana earned more money than she had in six years on the marathon tour. Diana trained with her usual fierce determination, but after failing in three different tries, she gave up the channel swim. After years at the top of a difficult sport, the thrill of marathon swimming was gone for Diana. She had faced and beaten seasickness, cold, and rough weather before. But she was afraid that something had happened to her all-important desire to touch the other shore, no matter what the cost.

Like the champion she is, however, within a few months Diana Nyad had taken on another challenge. She wanted to set one last record before she retired — a record so nearly impossible that it would stand for years to come. Diane decided to swim from Cuba to Florida — 130 miles, the longest open-water swim in history.

She began to train in July, 1977, a year before the swim. Diana ran ten to twelve miles a day. By December she could do twelve miles in seventy-two minutes. Twice a week she exercised with weight-training equipment, and she played squash an average of four hours a day. In March she switched from land to water training, swimming from five to eight hours a day. Diana moved to Florida in May for two months of ocean swimming, then spent two weeks resting and gaining weight for the swim.

She was ready to go in mid-July. But waiting for approval from the Cuban government delayed the swim until August 13, 1978. At 2:07 p.m. on Sunday, Diana Nyad waded into the waters off Cuba's Ortegosa Beach. "I guess I'll see you all in about two and a half days," she said.

Diana Nyad is shown in 1978 getting ready for her swim from Cuba to Florida.

Diana later described that Sunday night as the worst of her life. The wind blew all day at fifteen knots, and three- to four-foot waves smacked Diana from one side to another of her protective shark cage — built especially for her Cuba-Florida swim.

Poisonous jellyfish stung her arms and mouth, and her tongue was swollen to twice its normal size. Her hands, bleached white by the salt water, looked more like claws,

Forty-one hours and forty-seven minutes after leaving Cuba, Diana's trainers pulled her from the water. The wind had blown the bulky shark cage hopelessly off course. There was no way Diana could finish.

"But I can't quit," she said weakly when her trainer signalled her to stop. "Isn't there some other place to swim for?" A few minutes later she passed out.

Diana is convinced she could have made the swim on a decent day. Her crew agrees. "In early July, with no wind, she could swim to Key West, jump on the dock, and order a drink," said Bob Tittle, captain of one of the boats that followed Diana during her swim. And if Diana can get permission from the Cuban government, she will try the swim again.

Why? What makes a person put herself through the torture of becoming a great marathon swimmer? Diana describes herself as a person of extremes. "Every minute seems like the most important of my life," she says. "What interests me about marathon swimming is that it tests the human spirit. The real issue behind reaching the other shore is . . . the strength of the human will. When there is simply nothing left, you have to dig deeper and deeper into your gut until you arrive at a core of pride and dignity."

KITTY O'NEIL

*I guess I like danger and thrills. But mostly I want always to
have a goal, some dream that I can try for.*

Kitty O'Neil

"Wonder Woman, Move Over!" the headlines
shouted. "Here Comes Kitty O'Neil." Five feet,
three inches tall and weighing in at about 100
pounds, Kitty didn't exactly look the part. But by
December, 1976, there was no doubt that the
headlines were right.

Kitty O'Neil had already made a name for herself
as a champion diver, water skier, and motorcycle
racer. With less than a year's experience, she had
become one of Hollywood's top professional stunt

women. And on December 6, 1976, behind the wheel of a 48,000-horsepower car, she rocketed to a new women's land speed record and became the fastest woman on wheels.

Kitty has been totally deaf since the age of five months, when illness destroyed her hearing. Her father died in a plane crash not long after she was born, and her mother, a full-blooded Cherokee Indian, moved with Kitty to Wichita Falls, Texas. Patsy O'Neil went to the University of Texas to learn how to help her handicapped daughter. She taught Kitty to swim when Kitty was still a baby. Later, Kitty learned to speak and become an expert lip reader.

By the time she was eight, Kitty was ready to enter third grade in a regular, "hearing" school. She made good grades, took piano lessons, and learned to play the cello. Her sensitive fingers could "hear" even the smallest changes in tone by feeling the vibrations of the strings.

Kitty joined the school swim team when she was twelve. She excelled at the 100-meter freestyle, but her coach discouraged her from competing as a diver because she was deaf.

One day Kitty's team went to a swim meet in Oklahoma. One of the divers failed to appear. On a whim, Kitty asked to take the diver's place, and she walked away with a first-place gold medal. Years later she told a reporter, "I like to do things people say I can't do because I'm deaf."

Many more honors followed. Kitty won the 1961 AAU (Amateur Athletic Union) Southwest

District Junior Olympics diving title. At sixteen she moved to Anaheim, California, to train with Dr. Sammy Lee, a two-time Olympic diving champion.

Kitty trained at least four hours a day on the 10-meter (33 feet) diving board. Sometimes these sessions left her covered with bruises — painful reminders of mistimed dives. Still, she graduated with honors from Anaheim High School and went on to win the women's 10-meter diving championship at the AAU Nationals. Kitty broke her wrist at the Olympic qualifying trials but recovered soon enough to place eighth overall at the 1964 Tokyo Olympics. In 1967, she was training for the following year's Olympic team when spinal meningitis struck.

Doctors feared Kitty would never walk again. But she met this new challenge as she had every other one. Not only did she walk again — by 1970 she had added sky diving, scuba diving, and high speed sports car and drag boat racing to her list of experiences. In 1970, she set the world record for women's high speed water skiing — at 104.85 miles per hour.

In 1971, Kitty met Duffy Hambleton at a motorcycle meet in California. The two were married within a year. "She was unbelievable," Duffy said of his first meeting with Kitty. It astonished him that Kitty could race a bike without hearing the gears shift or the sounds of the other racers.

Mrs. Kitty O'Neil Hambleton settled into the role of a married woman for the next couple of

Kitty O'Neil is here performing a stunt for a TV show. She had to jump from the twelfth floor of a building.

years. She stayed in shape by lifting weights and running at least eight miles a day. But after a time she grew restless. Duffy was working regularly as a stunt man in movies and television so Kitty asked her husband to teach her the stunt business.

Kitty's training took two years. She began to stunt professionally in 1976 and quickly became one of the best in Hollywood.

"She's completely fearless," Duffy claims.

"I guess I like danger and thrills," Kitty told a reporter. "But mostly I want always to have a goal, some dream that I can try for."

It was not long before Kitty's next goal blasted into view. The sleek, 48,000-horsepower *Motivator* was the latest creation of Bill Fredrick, a pioneer designer and builder of high-speed cars. Fredrick wanted to break some records with his new jet car. Kitty agreed to go after the women's land speed record — 308.56 miles per hour — set by Lee Breedlove in 1965.

Test runs began in September, 1976. At California's El Mirage Dry Lake, Kitty set an unofficial women's record of 358 miles per hour. She needed a longer course to make it official, so in October the team moved to the Bonneville, Utah, salt flats. But the track was so rough that when Kitty reached 300 miles per hour, the *Motivator* started to waver all over the place. Kitty was fighting for her life in the struggle to control the land rocket.

On December 4, 1976, Kitty cracked the women's record with an official average speed of 322 miles per hour. She was the fastest women on wheels, but she wanted to go even faster. On December 6 she set an official record of 512.083 miles per hour — and she was using only sixty percent of the car's power. At one point during the run, the *Motivator* reached 600 miles per hour. It took Kitty five miles just to stop.

There seemed to be little doubt that Kitty could beat the overall land speed record in the *Motivator* — and maybe even approach the sound barrier. But there was one complicated problem that even Kitty's courage and determination couldn't change.

High-speed land racing is a costly business. It took more than $350,000 to develop and build the *Motivator*. And, it's not exactly an economy car. A short, five-mile trip burns up about $1,000 worth of the hydrogen-peroxide fuel the car runs on.

No one has yet broken the sound barrier on land. In both the 1977 and 1978 seasons, legal battles prevented the *Motivator* from trying again at Alvord.

In the meantime, Kitty O'Neil has had to content herself with the knowledge that she is the fastest women on earth, rather than the fastest person. If she gets the chance, however, she'll still go for a record of about 740 miles per hour, which just passes the speed of sound.

And, if she makes it, it won't be the first time that Kitty O'Neil has overcome a sound barrier. That first time came many years ago — with a great amount of work, courage, and determination.

ANNIE SMITH PECK

No one is acquainted with mountains who sees them only from valleys or from a railroad train . . . The wide expanse of earth and heaven, the stillness . . . calm and peace . . . these should attract and will charm every soul with a love of beauty.
Annie Smith Peck

In 1895, a forty-five year old former teacher became the first woman to climb the Matterhorn, a peak in the Alps that towers 14,685 feet (about 4,475 meters). She caused a sensation — not only by scaling the Matterhorn, but also because of her outspoken views on woman's equality, her gypsy lifestyle, and her unusual climbing costume. Newspaper photos of Annie Smith Peck — with boots, knickers, hip-length tunic and a soft, floppy hat tied on with a scarf — raised eyebrows across America.

41

Who was this woman? What would possess a teacher of Latin and Greek to change careers in the middle of her life and search for "some height where no *man* had stood before"?

Annie Smith Peck was born in Providence, Rhode Island, on October 19, 1850. Her parents were very proper people, a little on the stuffy side. Except for brother George, the family did not approve of Annie's mountain-climbing career.

Annie attended Dr. Stockbridge's School for Young Ladies and later the University of Michigan, where women could receive the same education as men. Annie earned a master's degree in 1881. By 1885 her reputation as a teacher and scholar enabled her to be the first woman admitted to the American School of Classical Studies in Athens, Greece.

About this same time, Annie discovered mountain climbing. "No one is acquainted with mountains who sees them only from valleys or from a railroad train," she later wrote. "The wide expanse of earth and heaven, the stillness . . . calm and peace . . . these should attract and will charm every soul with a love of beauty."

While traveling in Switzerland, in 1885, Annie had her first view of the Matterhorn. "I felt I should never be happy until I, too, should scale those frowning walls," she wrote. That year in Europe, Annie managed to climb several "little mountains." Then she returned to America to teach Latin at Smith College. She made her first important climb in 1888 — Mt. Shasta in California, only 300 feet (about 90 meters) shorter than the Matterhorn.

To earn extra money, so she could afford to travel, Annie began giving parlor lectures on Greek and Roman archaeology. By 1892 she had given up teaching to lecture and travel full-time.

On her second trip to Europe, Annie began to think mountain climbing might be a more popular lecture subject than ancient Greece and Rome. She tested her theory by climbing the peak that had captured her imagination ten years earlier. The excitement caused by her conquest of the Matterhorn proved she was right. But Annie was a little embarrassed by all the attention. Others had climbed the Matterhorn before her. She thought her newly won fame was "unmerited," and she wanted to do something to deserve it.

Mt. Orizaba in Mexico was the highest point anyone had reached in the Americas. But no one had ever determined just how high it was. Annie decided to measure it.

In 1897, she persuaded the New York *World* to send her to Mexico. The newspaper had a history of supporting adventurous women.

Thanks to the New York *World*, Annie's trek to the top of Orizaba was one of the few climbs for which she had enough money. She was successful on her first try and measured the mountain at 18,660 feet (5,688 meters). The climb set a world record for women.

After the conquest of Mt. Orizaba, Annie wanted to do "a little genuine exploration . . . to attain some height where no *man* had previously stood." No one had ever reached the top of Mt. Sorata in Bolivia, so she decided to try it. If the mountain measured more than 22,835 feet (6,960 meters), it would be higher than Aconcagua in Argentina, then thought to be the topmost point in the Western Hemisphere.

Annie set out in 1898 to raise money for the climb. She tried newspapers and magazines first, but none would pay the $5,000 she thought was needed. Next she went to individual people, asking each for $100. She raised a little money, but not nearly enough.

She finally set off on the climb — without enough money or skilled help. In 1904, after six years of struggle, she reached a height of 20,500 feet (6,248 meters). The climb broke the women's record she had set in Mexico in 1897.

But Annie Smith Peck still wanted to find a peak that was higher than Aconcagua. "Being always from my earliest years a firm believer in equality of the sexes," she wrote, "I felt that any great achievement . . . would be of advantage to my sex."

Mt. Huascarán in Peru was said to be 25,000 feet (about 7,600 meters). In 1904, Annie traveled there to map out approaches to its twin peaks. Two years of fund raising brought in barely enough money to cover her basic costs. Nonetheless, in 1906, Annie made two attempts to reach the top of Huascarán. Both attempts failed for lack of equipment and skilled guides.

Annie went back again in 1908. She was fifty-seven years old. On Friday, August 28, she set out on her sixth try for the summit of Huascarán.

44

Annie Smith Peck and three helpers are pictured on the deck of a ship with their mountain-climbing tools.

With her were two first-rate Swiss guides, Gabriel and Rudolph. Four Indian porters carried supplies.

At around 19,000 feet (about 5,800 meters), Annie and the two guides left the porters behind them for the last leg of the climb. High winds and unusual cold had made the climbing surface as smooth as glass. Still, they made good progress, and reached the top of the mountain around three o'clock in the afternoon.

Imagine Annie's disappointment and fury when Rudolph, one of the guides, actually set foot on the peak a few moments before she did. Worse still, high winds made it impossible for them to get an accurate reading of their height, though the guides estimated it at 24,000 feet (about 7,300 meters).

But Annie's frustration was nothing compared to her terror of the coming descent. Afterward she wrote, "My first thought on reaching the goal was, 'I am here at last, after all these years. But shall we ever get down?'"

The small toeholds that Gabriel had cut on the way up were dangerously hard to find on the way down — especially after dark. Both Annie and Rudolph slipped more than once. Gabriel later told Annie he thought the three would never return alive.

Finally, however, they reached safety. Annie and Gabriel were exhausted, but unharmed. Rudolph, however, suffered from extreme frostbite which caused the loss of most of his left hand, a finger of his right, and part of a foot. "His misfortune seemed indeed to outweigh any benefit derived from the ascent," Annie wrote.

Annie Smith Peck became an international celebrity after the climb. The president of Peru gave her a gold medal, and the North Peak of Huascarán was renamed Aña Peck in her honor. Annie vowed she would never again attempt such a climb without adequate funds and supplies.

The mountain was later measured at only 21,812 feet (6,648 meters). Annie had not smashed the world record for height. Still, she had climbed higher in the Western Hemisphere than any other American, male or female.

Annie continued to climb, explore, and write for the rest of her life. At sixty-one she became the first person to climb Mt. Coropuna in Peru. There she planted a "Votes for Women" pennant at the top. Annie lived to see American women win the right to vote in 1920.

Her last climb was in 1932. She scaled New Hampshire's Mt. Madison, which was about a mile (1.6 kilometers) high. It wasn't a bad showing for a woman of eighty-two. A couple of years later she set out on a tour of the world. Always a lover of the classics, she stopped in Athens, Greece, to climb the steep hill to the Acropolis.

Annie died a few months later at the age of eighty-five — "a humanist," according to the New York *Times*, "who could not leave the world without one more glimpse of the Parthenon."

BIBLIOGRAPHY

Bourke-White, Margaret. *Portrait of Myself*. New York: Simon & Schuster, 1963.

Brown, Theodore M. *Margaret Bourke-White: Photojournalist*. Ithaca, N.Y.: Cornell University, Andrew Dickson White Museum of Art, 1972.

Dolan, Edward F., and Lyttle, Richard B. *Janet Guthrie: First Woman Driver at Indianapolis*. Garden City, N.Y.: Doubleday & Co., 1978.

Gilfond, Henry. *Heroines of America*. New York: Fleet Press, 1970.

Guerin, Mrs. E.J. *Mountain Charley: or the Adventures of Mrs. E.J. Guerin, Who Was Thirteen Years in Male Attire*. Norman, Okla.: University of Oklahoma Press, 1968.

Nyad, Diana. *Other Shores*. New York: Random House, 1978.

Peck, Annie S. *A Search for the Apex of America: High Mountain Climbing in Peru and Bolivia*. New York: Dodd, Mead & Co., 1911.

Ross, Pat, ed. *Young and Female: Turning Points in the Lives of Eight American Women*. New York: Random House, 1972.